GRAND CANYON

A NATURAL WONDER OF THE WORLD

BY STEVEN L. WALKER

Above: Deciduous trees ablaze with fall colors stand in stark contrast to evergreen fir and pine at the base of a Coconino Sandstone formation near Point Imperial on the North Rim.
PHOTO BY GARY LADD

Front cover: Sunset at Mather Point on the South Rim of the Grand Canyon. Mather Point was named in honor of Stephen Tyng Mather (1867- 1930), the first director of the National Park Service.
PHOTO BY JERRY JACKA

Left: Sunrise over the eastern Grand Canyon from Cape Final on the North Rim.
PHOTO BY JEFF GNASS

Below: Sunrise over Wotan's Throne and Vishnu Temple from the Grand Canyon's South Rim. Many of the Canyon's formations were named after ancient gods by early visitors.
PHOTO BY GARY LADD

Designed by Camelback Design Group, Inc., 8655 East Via de Ventura, Suite G200, Scottsdale, Arizona 85258. Phone: 602-948-4233. Distributed by Canyonlands Publications, 4860 North Ken Morey Drive, Bellemont, Arizona 86015. For ordering information please call (520) 779-3888.

Requests for additional information should be made to: Camelback/Canyonlands Venture at the address above, or call our toll free telephone number: 1-800-283-1983.

Printed in South Korea
Library of Congress Catalog Number: 91-71501
International Standard Book Number: 1-879924-01-3

Published in the United States of America.

INTRODUCTION

The Grand Canyon is one of the Seven Natural Wonders of the World, keeping august company with Mount Everest in Nepal, Victoria Falls in Zimbabwe, the Great Barrier Reef in Australia, the cave paintings in France and Spain, the harbor at Rio de Janeiro in Brazil and Paricutin Volcano in Mexico. Although each of these natural wonders have been thoroughly studied and mapped, their immense dimensions and visual impact often defy comprehension when viewed for the first time. The Grand Canyon is certainly one of the most awe inspiring of these natural wonders.

To travel from one end of the Grand Canyon to the other requires a river journey of 277 miles. The distance between the walls of the North Rim and South Rim vary from less than one-half mile to 18 miles and the Canyon's depth reaches a maximum of almost 6000 feet. To travel from one side of the Canyon to the other requires an automobile trip of about 215 miles or a hike of 21 miles along steep trails. This hike takes the visitor through four of the seven life zones (regions sharing the same type of climate, plant and animal life) found on the North American Continent. This trek encompasses flora and fauna equivalent to that found on a trip from the Mexican desert to the Canadian woods.

Two billion years of geologic formations are exposed by the rock in the canyon walls. More geological evidence of the earth's history is on display at the Grand Canyon than can be found anywhere else. Each band of color on display in the Canyon's striated rock walls represents a unique set of geologic events of the earth's ancient past.

At the canyon floor, the Colorado River still carves deeper and deeper into ancient layers of rock formations. Prior to the construction of Glen Canyon Dam during the 1960s, the river removed an average of 400,000 tons of silt each day as it flowed through the Grand Canyon. The equivalent of 80,000 five-ton dump truck loads would be necessary to duplicate this immense task, at an average of one truck per second, twenty-four hours per day. Although the dam has greatly reduced the flow of the river at flood times from former levels, erosion of the Canyon by the Colorado River continues to carve the Canyon into the buried rock of the earth's past.

Standing at the Canyon's edge, one cannot help but feel an overwhelming sense of awe viewing nature's accomplishments. The early travelers to the area, when viewing the many large buttes rising from the Canyon's floor, were moved to name them after the ancient gods. Jupiter, Juno, Apollo, Venus, Vishnu, Deva, Shiva and Brahma have temples here, while Vulcan and Wotan have thrones. As these massive formations thrust upward from the bottom of the Canyon, they are framed by the colors and textures of the canyon walls.

ILLUSTRATION BY THOMAS MORAN

"Keep this great wonder of nature as it now is...Leave it as it is. You cannot improve on it; not a bit. The ages have been at work on it, and man can only mar it. What you can do is keep it for your children, your children's children, and for all who come after you, as the one great sight which every American, if he can travel at all, should see."

President Theodore Roosevelt, 1903

Preceding pages: A storm builds over the South Rim of the Grand Canyon. The lower elevations of the South Rim experience significantly less rain and snowfall than the higher elevations of the Canyon's North Rim.
PHOTO BY LARRY ULRICH

Left: View of Mount Hayden from Point Imperial on the North Rim. Mount Hayden is formed of Coconino Sandstone resting on red Hermit Shale.
PHOTO BY DICK DIETRICH

Right: Twilight settles over the Colorado Butte and the eastern Grand Canyon.
PHOTO BY JEFF GNASS

INTRODUCTION CONTINUED...

The Paiutes believed the Canyon had been constructed by the god Tavwoats to separate the world of the living from the lands beyond death. It was said he filled the Canyon with the raging waters of the Colorado River so the people could not escape the woes of the present world for the pleasures of the next. The Hulapai and the Havasupai believed the river was the runoff of an earth covering flood, much the same as the one Noah experienced.

The first Europeans to visit the Canyon, Spanish conquistadors under the leadership of Don Garcia Lopez de Cardenas, were not impressed by its natural wonders. In search of material wealth and the Seven Cities of Gold, they spent four days vainly searching for a path to the bottom of the Canyon to acquire water they desperately needed. They were unable to reach the Colorado River below and left empty handed and uninspired. It was another 200 years before the Spaniards were to return to the Canyon.

The first Americans to visit the region, an army survey party in search of a southern supply route to Utah, found the locale "profitless" and wrote disparaging reports regarding the Canyon's value. It was not until the famous voyage of John Wesley Powell, in 1869, that Americans took an active interest in exploring the Grand Canyon.

Today millions of visitors from around the world visit the Grand Canyon each year, each leaving with a sense of enrichment that is at once personal, but yet universal, in terms of fulfillment. To experience the Grand Canyon is to commune with nature at her very finest.

Right: Sundown in winter at Hopi Point.
PHOTO BY JERRY SIEVE

Below: The Colorado River winds through Marble Canyon at Nankoweap.
PHOTO BY TOM TILL

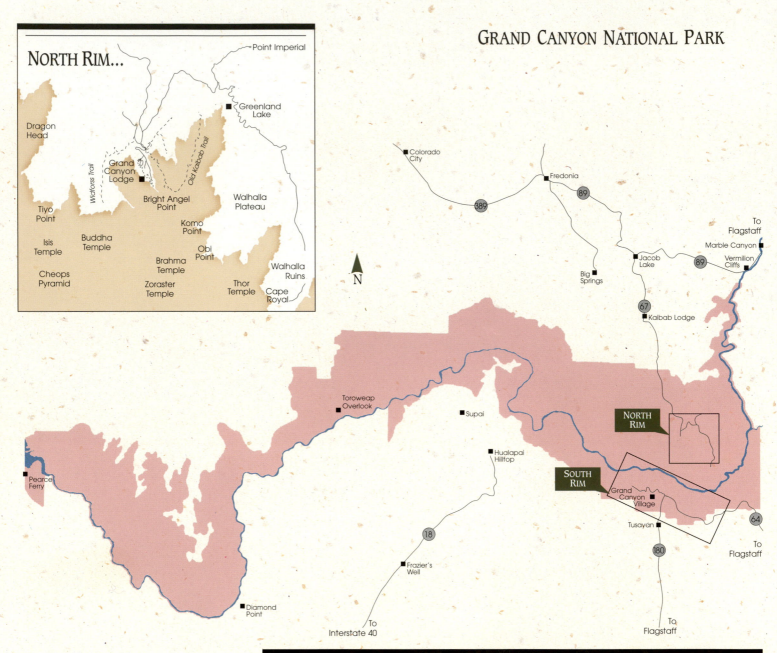

NORTH RIM...

Point Imperial · Dragon Head · Greenland Lake · Grand Canyon Lodge · Widforss Trail · Old Kaibab Trail · Bright Angel Point · Walhalla Plateau · Tiyo Point · Komo Point · Isis Temple · Buddha Temple · Obi Point · Cheops Pyramid · Brahma Temple · Walhalla Ruins · Zoraster Temple · Thor Temple · Cape Royal

Colorado City · Fredonia · 389 · 89 · To Flagstaff · Marble Canyon · Big Springs · Jacob Lake · 89 · Vermilion Cliffs · 67 · Kaibab Lodge · NORTH RIM · Toroweap Overlook · Supai · Hualapai Hilltop · SOUTH RIM · Grand Canyon Village · Pearce Ferry · Tusayan · 64 · 18 · 180 · To Flagstaff · Frazier's Well · To Flagstaff · Diamond Point · To Interstate 40 · N

Distances from Grand Canyon Visitor's Center to popular western United States destinations by automobile. Distances are approximate.

DESTINATION	MILES	KILOMETERS
Albuquerque, NM	401	646
Death Valley, CA	432	696
Denver, CO	846	1362
Flagstaff, AZ	80	129
Hoover Dam	240	386
Jacob Lake, AZ	174	280
Kingman, AZ	178	287
Las Vegas, NV	280	799
Los Angeles, CA	496	799
North Rim	215	346
Phoenix, AZ	226	364
Salt Lake City, UT	663	1068
San Diego, CA	523	842
San Francisco, CA	833	1341
Tucson, AZ	338	544
Williams,az	60	97
Zion NP, UT	253	407

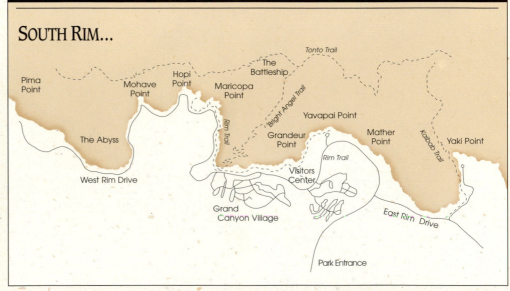

SOUTH RIM...

Tonto Trail · The Battleship · Pima Point · Hopi Point · Mohave Point · Maricopa Point · Bright Angel Trail · Yavapai Point · The Abyss · Rim Trail · Grandeur Point · Mather Point · Kaibab Trail · Yaki Point · West Rim Drive · Visitors Center · Rim Trail · Grand Canyon Village · East Rim Drive · Park Entrance

GEOGRAPHY

The Colorado River flows for more than 277 miles through the canyons encompassing Grand Canyon National Park from Lee's Ferry, located near the junction of the Paria and the Colorado rivers in northern Arizona, to the western border that Arizona shares with Nevada, near Pearce Ferry. Grand Canyon National Park covers approximately 1900 square miles of the Colorado Plateau physiographic province, which in turn covers 130,000 square miles of parts of Arizona, Utah, Colorado and New Mexico.

The distance between the North Rim and South Rim of the Canyon varies from less than one-half mile to 18 miles. The Canyon reaches a maximum depth of almost 6000 feet. The difference in elevations between the North and South rims vary up to 1200 feet in the developed areas and as much as 2000 feet in undeveloped areas. Point Imperial at the North Rim, with an elevation of 8803 feet, is the highest view point within the Canyon proper, although one spot near the park's northern boundary reaches 9165 feet. The deepest area of the Canyon's chasm is around 1200 feet above sea level. The South Rim reaches its highest point at 7500 feet and Grand Canyon Village attains an altitude of 6886 feet.

The wide range in elevations at the Grand Canyon allows an equally wide range of landscapes, climates, flora and fauna. Four of the seven life zones found on the North American continent can be found within the park. Steep vertical walls of the Canyon contain several distinct zones of physical and biological environments with climates that range from subarctic to desert.

Rainfall in the Canyon also has a wide range depending upon location, from an average 8.5 inches at Phantom Ranch, at the Canyon floor, to more than 25 inches annually on the North Rim. The South Rim receives less than 16 inches in a typical year. Snowfall on the North Rim averages more than 128 inches annually, less than 65 inches on the South Rim and less than one inch in the Inner Canyon.

Summer temperatures may reach 115° along the Canyon floor while rarely exceeding 80° at the North Rim. The South Rim seldom sees temperatures greater than 90°. Winter temperatures are also affected by the difference in elevations with the Inner Canyon remaining as much as 20° warmer than those along the Canyon's rims.

The North Rim features mountain meadows in shallow valleys of spruce and fir. Winter snows remain late in the year and abundant rainfall provide sufficient moisture for a burgeoning rebirth of wildflowers in spring and summer. As the elevation of the North Rim decreases, Spruce-Fir biotic communities are replaced by ponderosa pine forests and in some places dips low enough to feature piñon and juniper woodland communities. This shift

The Grand Canyon, located on the Colorado Plateau in northern Arizona, covers 1900 square miles and has elevations ranging from 1200 to 9100 feet. The wide range in altitude provides for a variety of landscape, flora, fauna and climate.

Preceding pages: Mount Hayden, named for Arizona pioneer Charles Trumbull Hayden, as viewed from above the clouds at Point Imperial on the North Rim of the Grand Canyon.
PHOTO BY DICK DIETRICH

Right: Vishnu Temple, one of several buttes in the Grand Canyon named after ancient gods, as viewed from Cape Royal on the North Rim.
PHOTO BY BOB CLEMENZ

in flora and fauna is due in part to decreasing elevations and in part to climactic effects in the Canyon as warm, dry air rises from the depths of the Canyon's floor to the rims.

The South Rim is predominantly piñon and juniper woodland with ponderosa pine limited to small, protected sites on hillsides and along washes. With significantly lighter snowfall in winter than the North Rim, and less rain in spring and summer, South Rim landscapes are mostly open, low woodland.

Spring arrives earlier to the South Rim than to the North and most of its flora species bloom as much as a month earlier than their counterparts on the North Rim. As summer enters July, afternoon thunderstorms bring much needed moisture to the South Rim and often a second flowering season. Fall and winter arrive earlier in the higher elevations of the North Rim.

The driest, and hottest, area of the Canyon is the Inner Canyon. As one descends from the rim, piñon and juniper prevail with trees gradually becoming smaller and sparser, as the trail descends to the 3000 foot level where desert flora begins to emerge. Here, cacti and low shrubs are predominant, forming a stark contrast to the flora of the rims above. With a vertical descent of only one mile, the visitor can travel the equivalent distance, in terms of life zones (flora, fauna and climates), of a trip from the Mexican border to the Rocky Mountains of central Canada.

HAVASU CANYON

ELEVATIONS ALONG THE RIMS...

The dramatic changes in elevations along the Grand Canyon's North and South Rims, varying as much as 2000 feet at their highest elevations and more between high points and low areas, create environments with climates ranging from desert to subarctic.

This variety in elevations and climates allows a range of landscapes, flora and fauna. Four of seven life zones found on the North American Continent– Canadian, Transition, Upper Sonoran and Low Sonoran– can be found, along with their characteristic flora, fauna and climates.

Point Imperial, with an elevation of 8803 feet on the North Rim, is the highest point within the Canyon proper although one area near the park's northern boundary reaches 9165 feet. The deepest area within the Canyon's chasm is approximately 1200 feet above sea level. The South Rim reaches its highest point at 7500 feet and Grand Canyon Village, the center of most accommodations at the Canyon, attains an elevation of 6886 feet. The depth of the Canyon from the South Rim, near the village, to the Canyon's floor is approximately one mile.

U.S. PROFILE

SIERRA NEVADA

ROCKY MOUNTAINS

U.S. CANYON DEPTHS

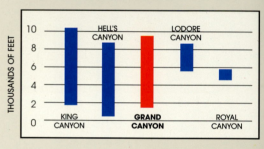

CLIMATE

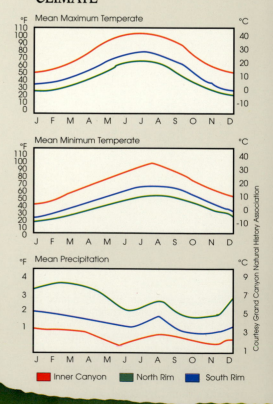

Courtesy Grand Canyon Natural History Association

MAP OF THE EASTERN GRAND CANYON

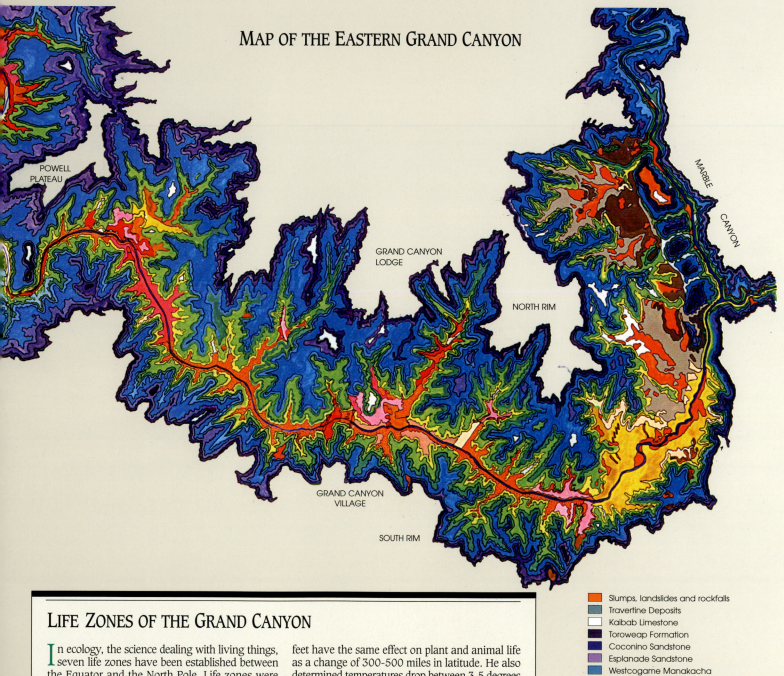

POWELL
PLATEAU

MARBLE
CANYON

GRAND CANYON
LODGE

NORTH RIM

GRAND CANYON
VILLAGE

SOUTH RIM

Legend

- Slumps, landslides and rockfalls
- Travertine Deposits
- Kaibab Limestone
- Toroweap Formation
- Coconino Sandstone
- Esplanade Sandstone
- Westcogame Manakacha and Watahomigi
- Redwall Limestone
- Muav Limestone
- Bright Angel Shale
- Tapeats Sandstone
- Kwagunt Formation
- Galeros Formation
- Cardenas Lava
- Dox Sandstone
- Hakatai Shale
- Granite to Grandodiorite
- Grandodiorite to Quartz Diorite
- Predominately Diabase Intrusives
- Predominately Schist
- Predominately Amphibolite

LIFE ZONES OF THE GRAND CANYON

In ecology, the science dealing with living things, seven life zones have been established between the Equator and the North Pole. Life zones were established by Clinton Hart Merriam during the late 1800s early 1900s. Merriam based his study on the premise that changes in elevation of 1000 feet have the same effect on plant and animal life as a change of 300-500 miles in latitude. He also determined temperatures drop between 3-5 degrees for each 1000 foot rise in elevation. The Grand Canyon is home to four life zones: the Canadian, Transition, Upper Sonoran and Lower Sonoran.

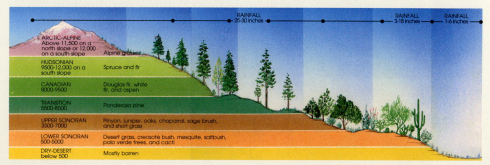

GREAT PLAINS

APPALACHIAN HIGHLANDS

GEOLOGY

Trilobites, small crab-like creatures found fossilized within the Tapeats Sandstone formation, are testimony that sea life existed in the Grand Canyon region during the Cambrian period of the Paleozoic era.

The Grand Canyon has been shaped by the passage of time and the ravages of nature. The region was at times covered by seas, rivers have cut deep gorges through surface strata, and earthquakes have bent, twisted, dropped and folded the land. Volcanic eruptions have spewed lava and ash and the land suffered through innumerable droughts. Fortunately, these forces occurred over the last four billion years. Had they all occurred at the same time, the area surely would have been hell on earth.

There is no better place to study the formation of the earth than at the Grand Canyon. From the Canyon's rims, visitors may gaze down through as much as 6250 feet of rock formations, more geological history than is displayed anywhere else in the world. From the Paleozoic era rims to the bottom of the Precambrian era Inner Canyon, nearly two billion years of geological history are exposed.

During the last million years, the Colorado River has cut its course through the Canyon's walls and has exposed a fossil record of the earth that dates to the first living organisms—sea life imprinted in rock that resemble jellyfish. As succeeding layers of rock formations progress up the Canyon walls, fossils imbedded within tell the story of the changes in the earth since its beginning.

The 1900 square miles of Grand Canyon National Park, and the 130,000 square miles of the Colorado Plateau in which it resides, are the most unique of the thirty-four natural regions comprising the United States. In this region, extensive areas of horizontal strata of sedimentary rocks, which have been exposed by the Colorado River and layered on top of one another, share the plateau with igneous rocks from volcanoes, cinder cones and lava flows. Structural upheavals created striking topographic features and the high base altitude of the Colorado Plateau. The plateau's general surface area has an elevation of more higher than 5000 feet and some subplateaus, and several peaks at the nearby San Francisco Peaks, reach up to 11,000 feet. This uplifting, coupled with the brightly colored and highly varied scenery, make the region one of the most unusual places in the world.

Geology is the scientific study of the origin, history and structure of the earth. All studies are based on the division and sub-division of historical geology into eras, periods and epochs. The Precambrian era includes all geologic time up to 600 million years ago; the Paleozoic era, from 600 million to 225 million years ago; the Mesozoic era, from 225 million to 65 million years ago; and the Cenozoic era, the last 65 million years. Each of these past ages are in turn divided into time segments called periods which are further defined by epochs. The rocks of these different ages, when exposed as in the walls of the Grand Canyon, form the basis for

Left: The North Rim, with elevations between 1000 and 2000 feet higher than the South Rim, supports plant and animal communities not found in other areas of the Grand Canyon.
PHOTO BY DICK DIETRICH

Right: Sunrise over the Inner Gorge at Toroweap Point in the western Grand Canyon.
PHOTO BY JEFF GNASS

the study to gain geologic knowledge of the past history of the earth.

Because of the long length of time allotted to the the Precambrian era, it is divided into two periods– late and early. Earlier Precambrian rocks, which form the walls of the Inner Gorge, can be easily identified from the rim of the Grand Canyon. In places, these rocks rise as much as 1500 feet above the level of the Colorado River.

Most of the rock formations of the early Precambrian were laid in horizontal layers, while others had intrusions of volcanic materials. Once, these formations were thousands of feet thick, the earth's crust folded, buckled and was warped by tremendous internal forces and a complete range of mountains was created. Extreme heat and pressure was generated in the rocks as movements in the earth occurred, the rocks crystallized and were metamorphosed. The dark metamorphic rocks are Vishnu Schist and the lighter rocks in this strata are Zoroaster Granite.

As Early Precambrian mountains eroded, the region was covered by water during the Late Precambrian. Sediments in the water built the formations of the Late Precambrian inch by inch. The lowest formation, Bass Limestone, was deposited directly on the surface of the Vishnu Schist. This layer features primitive plants and algae and represents the oldest forms of life found in the rocks of the Canyon.

On this formation lies Hakatai Shale, which was formed under water. This layer also contains Shinumo Quartzite, deposits of tightly cemented quartz-sand grains, and the Dox formation, which are also sedimentary. Molten rock from deep within the earth was thrust upward into these sedimentary layers, forming sills and dikes, and occasionally reaching the surface as basalt flows.

As layers of rock formations accumulated,

the total thickness of the Late Precambrian period reached more than 12,000 feet. Once again, pressures from within the earth uplifted mountains, these being fault-block in nature, and during the millions of years of the Late Precambrian they were eroded, leaving only a plain, with ridges of resistant rocks remaining. These formations may be seen along the South Kaibab and North Kaibab trails and to the west of Grand Canyon Village.

Paleozoic era formations cover the upper two-thirds of the Canyon walls. During this period the region was covered by the sea and river flood plains, affected by periods of great drought, and covered by desert sand dunes. These different periods of erosional activity produced several unconformities, or gaps, in the record revealed by the Canyon's walls.

The base of the Paleozoic era was formed of Tapeats Sandstone deposited along outside margins of an ancient sea that covered the exposed layers of Early Precambrian strata. This contact between the Tapeats Sandstone and Early Precambrian deposits is called the Great Unconformity because the time required for the rocks of the Late Precambrian period to be deposited, elevated into fault-block mountains, and finally be eroded away, represents a gap in the record of as much as 1.2 billion years. Tapeats Sandstone is composed of different strata ranging from course pebbles to fine sand and reaches a thickness of up to 300 feet. Ripple marks, trilobite trails and tubeworm burrows give testimony to the presence of the sea during formation of these deposits.

Above the Tapeats formation lies the Bright Angel Shale formation, comprised of greenish

Below: Gazing down from the Kaibab Limestone formations of the North Rim as much as 6250 feet of exposed rock formations are visible, more exposed geology than anywhere else on earth.
PHOTO BY JEFF GNASS

siltstone and shale. This layer also includes varieties of primitive shellfish and trilobites (small crab-like creatures), that inhabited the seas for millions of years.

Above the Bright Angel Shale formation, which reaches a thickness of up to 450 feet, lies the Muav Limestone formation. The Muav formation reaches thicknesses of up to 1000 feet, acting as a regional aquifer with springs emerging from the Canyon walls. In places above the Muav Limestone formation there exists another unconformity which dates from 400 to 500 million years ago. This unconformity occurred after a period of erosion and after the Muav formation emerged from the sea. Cracks formed by this erosion process were filled with another sedimentary deposit from advancing seas called Temple Butte Limestone. In this strata fossils have been found with bony plates, or scales, as armored fish, and others with backbones have been discovered. Corrals and brachiopods, primitive shellfish, have also been identified.

The next formation to be deposited was the Redwall Limestone formation, which reaches a thickness of up to 700 feet. Redwall Limestone is actually gray in color, but has been stained by iron oxide washed down from the Supai Group deposits above. In places where the Supai Group has been completely eroded away, the Redwall Limestone weathers to its natural gray color.

The Supai Group is actually four separate, but similar, formations deposited as the seas retreated leaving a limy lower strata. Upper

Above: Lava Falls at the Colorado River. At one time this lava flow dammed the river, forming a lake miles up the Canyon.
PHOTO BY LARRY ULRICH

deposits were formed of sand deposited by ancient rivers. Although no traces of four-footed animal bones have been found, there are tracks of such creatures evident in the exposed rock. These tracks are pressed deep into the rock and show evidence of a dragging tail. Because the footprints are close together, scientists surmise that they were made by creatures resembling today's crocodiles, or alligators, with their characteristic heavy bodies and short legs.

Above the Supai Group, which reaches a thickness of nearly 1350 feet, are deposits of Hermit Shale, which were deposited by fresh-water streams leaving mud and clay behind. Iron deposits present in the Hermit Shale formation give it a deep red color. Fossils in the Hermit Shale include those of ferns, insects and coniferous (cone bearing) plants. Hermit Shale reaches a thickness of up to 1000 feet.

Coconino Sandstone lies atop the Hermit Shale and gives evidence of desert sand dunes compressed into sandstone as a warm, shallow

Above: The Great Unconformity, shown here at Conquistador Aisle in Blacktail Canyon, results in a gap in the geologic record that may be as much as 1.2 billion years.
PHOTO: LARRY ULRICH

sea filled the area; eroded away the tops of the dunes; and added the necessary pressure to turn the sand to sandstone. This encroaching sea deposited the Toroweap formation, which has red and yellow sandstone at its top and bottom with a layer of gray limestone in its middle. The Toroweap formation reaches a thickness of up to 450 feet.

Once again, sea water flooded the Grand Canyon and the Kaibab Sea advanced into the region, leaving behind a 300 foot deposit of

Left: Vulcan's Throne, a large cinder cone, rises 567 feet above the Esplanade. Vulcan's Throne was formed within the last 20,000 years.
PHOTO BY DICK DIETRICH

Kaibab Limestone. This is the top formation visible at the rim of the Canyon. This creamy-white limestone rock contains corals, sea-lilies, brachiopods, sponges and shark teeth. The Kaibab formation was deposited at the end of the Paleozoic era. Although it was below sea level when deposited, they reach elevations of 9000 feet, or more, today.

Above: Clear Creek cascades through Vishnu Schist in Granite Gorge. Vishnu Schist dates from the Early Precambrian era and is at least 1.7 billion years old.
PHOTO: LARRY ULRICH

Rock formations of the Mesozoic era at one time completely covered the Grand Canyon region, although most have been completely eroded away. The Mesozoic was known as the "Age of the Reptiles," a time when dinosaurs roamed the earth. All that remains in evidence of the Mesozoic era are remnants left behind, such as Cedar Mountain, Red Butte and the Vermilion Cliffs. The cliffs to the north of the Grand Canyon, in Southern Utah, were carved during the Mesozoic era but survived because they did not face the same forces of erosion as those in the Grand Canyon region.

The Cenozoic era found the region above sea level for the first time. The dominant forces of the Cenozoic era were the widespread erosional forces that completely stripped away the Mesozoic era deposits and, during the last several million years, have carved the Grand Canyon through the rock formations from the

Right: Zoraster Granite at Deer Creek Falls is Precambrian and probably extends, along with Vishnu Schist, thousands of feet below the floor of the Grand Canyon.
PHOTO: BY LARRY ULRICH

Paleozoic and Precambrian eras.

During the last two million years, volcanic activity occurred in the Grand Canyon region. Molten rock was spewed from the depths of the earth. Volcanoes appeared and lava flows poured down the Canyon walls, in some places damming the river to form lakes. Volcanic activity occurred in the region during several different periods during the late Cenozoic era. Lava flowed into the Canyon at least ten times during the past million years, creating flows in Prospect Canyon, Whitmore Wash and at Toroweap Valley which dammed the Colorado River. The largest dam was around 1400 feet high and created a lake that backed up the Canyon for 150 miles. The most recent eruption in the area occurred at Sunset Crater, near the San Francisco Peaks, in 1064 AD.

Above: A detail of Vishnu Schist. The sculptured appearance of this Vishnu Schist was caused by water erosion called "stream fluting."
PHOTO BY TOM TILL

ROCK NAME

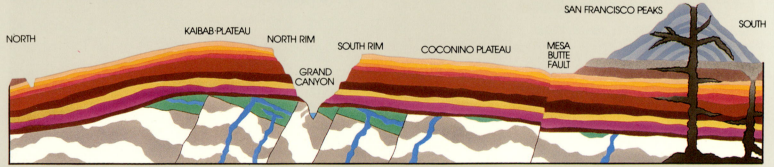

Rock Name	THICKNESS (In Feet)	DEPOSITIONAL ENVIRONMENT	AGE (millions of years)	GEOLOGIC TIME Era	Period
KAIBAB LIMESTONE	300-500	SEA	250		Middle Permian
TOROWEAP FORMATION	250-450	SEA	260		Middle Permian
COCONINO SANDSTONE	50-350	DESERT	270		Early Permian
HERMIT SHALE	250-1,000	FLOODPLAIN	280	PALEOZOIC	Early Permian
SUPAI GROUP	950-1,350	SWAMP	300		Pennsylvanian
REDWALL LIMESTONE	450-700	SEA	330		Early and Middle Mississippian
TEMPE BUTTE LIMESTONE	30-1,000	SEA	370		Late Devonian
	DISCONFORMITY		400-500		Silurian and Orodovician
MUAV LIMESTONE	50-1,000	SEA	530		Middle Cambrian
BRIGHT ANGEL SHALE	200-450	SEA	540		Early and Middle Cambrian
TAPEATS SANDSTONE	100-300	SEA	550		Early Cambrian
	THE GREAT UNCONFORMITY		570-800		
GRAND CANYON SUPERGROUP	15,000	SEA	800-1,200	PRECAMBRIAN	Late
VISHNU SCHIST		Metamorphosed Sea Sediments	1,700		Early
ZOROASTER GRANITE		Molten Intrusion			

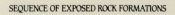

SEQUENCE OF EXPOSED ROCK FORMATIONS

GEOLOGIC CROSS SECTION OF THE GRAND CANYON REGION

Although the epic production that created the Grand Canyon began more than 2 billion years ago, the last 4 million years has shown the most significant changes to the surface topography.

2 billion years ago: Volcanic materials and sediments accumulated.

1.7 billion years ago: As the mountains were uplifted, rocks metamorphosed into Vishnu Schist.

1.5 billion years ago: Erosion brought the mountains to a nearly level plain.

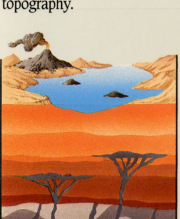

1.2 billion years ago: As the plain subsided the Grand Canyon Supergroup layers were deposited.

800 million years ago: Fault block mountains were formed.

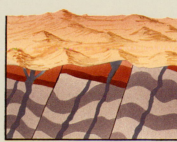

700 million years ago: The fault block mountains eroded into hilly topography.

600 million years ago: The area subsided and Paleozoic layers were deposited.

230 million years ago: Mesozoic sediments were deposited.

65 million years ago: Faulting activity uplifted the Mesozoic.

4 million years ago: The Colorado River began to cut its path.

These ten major, large scale geological events worked together, over the last 2 billion years, to form what is the Grand Canyon today. The actual date each event occurred can only be approximated by the evidence found in the exposed rocks of the canyon's walls.

Below: The Colorado River surges through House Rock Rapids in Marble Canyon.
PHOTO BY JIM COWLIN

HISTORY

Discovery of the Grand Canyon by the first Europeans in the region began on a less than auspicious note. Incredibly, early explorers of the region found it to be less than noteworthy and of no economic value. In 1540, Francisco Vasques de Coronado, the Spanish conquistador, led the first expedition of Europeans through the territory which was then called New Spain. Coronado– along with 336 other Spaniards, 1000 Indian allies, 1500 horses and mules, and numerous cattle and sheep– had ventured north from Mexico in search of the legendary Seven Cities of Cibola, which were also referred to as the "Cities of Gold" in myths of the day.

On August 25, 1540, Coronado sent 25 men, under the command of Captain Garcia Lopez de Cardenas, north to the lands of the Colorado Plateau to investigate rumors of a large river and Indians who possessed great wealth. After great hardships and disappointing results in the early months of the search, Garcia's party finally reached the Grand Canyon at an area probably on the South Rim. They found neither the gold they were seeking, nor reached the river at the bottom of the Canyon. They failed to even name the giant abyss.

After their futile attempts to locate the great sources of wealth of the legends, the Spaniards passed exploration of the territory from the conquistadors to the Franciscan missionaries. This act itself was a testament to the lack of regard the Spanish held for the Grand Canyon.

Indeed, it was more than 200 years later, in 1776, that the next Spaniard, Father Francisco Tomas Garces, visited the area. Father Garces descended into Havasu Canyon and became the first European to reach the Colorado River.

Foraging for food on the long expedition to the Grand Canyon had proven unsuccessful for Father Garces' company and they were forced to eat two of their horses during their stay at the Canyon. Garces gave the Canyon its first European name, "Puerto de Bucareli," or "Bucareli Pass," in honor of Antonio Maria de Bucareli y Ursua, the viceroy of New Spain.

The Colorado River was first named by the Spaniards in 1539, when Francisco de Ulloa, commanding three ships, sailed to the river's mouth at the head of the Gulf of California. Again, the first Spanish explorer to gaze upon what today is considered a natural wonder did not even bother to name his discovery.

The following year Hernando de Alarcorn sailed to the river's mouth and named it "El Rio de Buena Guia," or the "River of Good Guidance." The same year, Spaniard Melchior Diaz journeyed to the river, naming it "Rio del Tison," or "Firebrand River," after the torches carried by local Indians.

The Colorado River was renamed yet again in 1604 by Juan de Onate, the Spanish governor of New Mexico. He called the river "Rio de Buena Esperanza," which translates as "The River of Good Hope." As the 1600s continued, the river was generally became known as "Rio

Early exploration of the Grand Canyon by Spanish conquistadors was less than successful. The first party of Spaniards to reach the region were in search of the "Seven Cities of Gold." They were unable to locate the mineral wealth they were seeking and were unsuccessful in discovering a route to the Colorado River, which they could see from the Canyon rim, to obtain water they so desperately needed.

Preceding pages: Sunset over the South Rim of the Grand Canyon from Yaki Point.
PHOTO BY DICK DIETRICH

Left: The Colorado River flowing tranquilly through Conquistador Aisle.
PHOTO BY LARRY ULRICH

Right: A spring storm at sunset from Transept Canyon on the North Rim.
PHOTO BY DAVID ELMS, JR.

Colorado del Norte", meaning the "Red River of the North."

Father Eusebio Francisco Kino, an explorer and Jesuit priest, drew the first map in 1701, labeling the river *Rio Colorado del Norte*. A name since anglicized to its present form, the Colorado River.

The mouth of Black Canyon from the 1857 expedition of Joesph Christmas Ives.

The Grand Canyon did not receive its present name until well into the 1850s, prior to which it was referred to as the "Big Cañon" and "Grand Cañon of the Colorado." Cañon is the Spanish spelling of Canyon. By 1868, the name "Grand Canyon" had generally taken hold and began to appear on maps of the region.

After cursory exploration of the Canyon by the Spanish, control of the area passed from the Spaniards to the Mexicans in 1821. During this time American fur trappers began frequenting the Canyon in search of beaver pelts.

In 1826, James Ohio Pattie visited the region, later writing his famous *Personal Narrative*.

During 1828, George C. Yount led a trapping party into the Canyon which was reported to have reached the floor of the western end of the Grand Canyon by making a descent from Spencer Canyon to the river below.

Dr. John S. Newberry, the geologist for Lt. Joesph Christmas Ives' expedition.
PHOTO COURTESY GRAND CANYON NATIONAL PARK I.D. NO. 3332

In 1848, war between Mexico and the United States ended with the signing of the Treaty of Guadalupe Hidalgo. The Grand Canyon, along with the territories of New Mexico, Arizona, Texas and California, became part of the United States. This change in ownership did little to promote the territory until President James Buchanan called for regional surveys in 1857.

As friction developed between the Mormons of Utah and the federal government in the late 1850s, Pres. Buchanan ordered army troops to the Southwest to quell what he feared was a state of open rebellion by Mormons. To insure federal control of the territory, the president ordered the U.S. Army to find a southern route of supply to the troops in Utah. The army sent Lt. Joseph C. Ives of the Corps of Topographical Engineers, to find the northernmost point of steamship navigation on the lower Colorado River. Ives established this at a point in Black

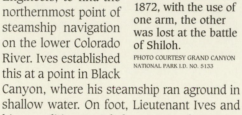

Major John Wesley Powell traversed the Grand Canyon by boat in 1869, and in 1872, with the use of one arm, the other was lost at the battle of Shiloh.
PHOTO COURTESY GRAND CANYON NATIONAL PARK I.D. NO. 5133

Canyon, where his steamship ran aground in shallow water. On foot, Lieutenant Ives and his expedition traveled on to Peach Springs where they descended into the Canyon and followed Diamond Creek north to the Colorado River. They finally arrived at the Grand Canyon in April of 1858.

After examination of the region by members of the expedition, Lieutenant Ives found little strategic value to the Grand Canyon. Lt. Ives then continued his journey to Fort Defiance where he entered in his report that the Grand Canyon was "valueless," much the same as his Spanish predecessors had written.

Lieutenant Ives stated in his official report to his superiors in Washington, D.C., "Ours has been the first, and will doubtless be the last, party of whites to visit this profitless locality."

Although Lieutenant Ives personally found little of economic or strategic value to the Grand Canyon, with him on his expedition was Dr. John Strong Newberry. Through his written reports on the geology of the Grand Canyon, Dr. Newberry became the first white man to be known to contemplate the geology of the Grand Canyon and to question its forma-

Benjamin Harrison, the 34th President of the United States, designated the Grand Canyon a Forest Reserve in 1893.
COURTESY NATIONAL ARCHIVES

tions. Dr. Newberry wrote of physical features of the canyons, rocks and fossils concluding that the Colorado River had eroded the Grand Canyon. These written reports were the first by an academic to discuss geological formation of features of the Grand Canyon.

The Mormon uprising failed to create a major incident. In the following years small groups of prospectors roamed the area in searching for mineral wealth. Like the earlier conquistadors, it

President Woodrow Wilson signed the bill responsible for creating Grand Canyon National Park in 1919.
COURTESY NATIONAL ARCHIVES

is highly probable that their search for gold and silver kept them from noticing the natural beauty of the area.

It was not until after the famous river voyage of John Wesley Powell, in 1869, that the Grand Canyon began to attract visitors for its beauty alone. Powell, a former Union Army major who had lost an arm during the battle of Shiloh in the Civil War, undertook a bold and imaginative expedition to prove it was possible to navigate the Colorado River by boat along the entire length of the Grand Canyon.

Powell's well written accounts of his amazing journey spurred the imaginations of readers, then and now, and was a key factor in the continuing interest that developed in the Grand Canyon and the Colorado Plateau.

In 1870, Major Powell explored the northern areas of the Colorado Plateau while planning a second expedition down the Colorado River. This time, in the spring of 1871, Major Powell was sent by the federal government to map the Colorado Plateau and the Colorado River. It is interesting to note that Powell, although retired from the Union Army, was a promoter for profit in all of the expeditions he undertook. Without sponsorship from the government, and the private sector, Major Powell would

THE VOYAGE OF JOHN WESLEY POWELL

Major John Wesley Powell, a retired Union Army officer who lost his right arm at the battle of Shiloh in the Civil War, was not a man known to let hardship and adversity deter him in his quest for adventure. Powell, who had a strong background in the study of natural sciences, particularly geology, set out to traverse the Colorado River through the Grand Canyon by boat on May 24, 1869.

He embarked on his now famous voyage from Green River, Wyoming (see map) and concluded it at the Virgin River, more than 1000 miles away. Major Powell chose Green River for its railhead on the Union Pacific Railroad, which had reached the area a few years before. The railhead enabled Powell's expedition a means of easy transportation for the necessary supplies, not to mention four pine boats, to the starting point of the journey.

Major Powell descended the Green River to the Colorado River with nine men in the four pine boats. On the first leg of the journey one of the boats was destroyed and one member of the expedition declared he had seen enough danger and quit the expedition.

The Powell expedition continued down the Colorado River through Cataract Canyon and Glen Canyon and finally entered the Grand Canyon. While in the Grand Canyon, at what is now known as Separation Rapid, three more men decided it was unsafe to continue and left the river to find an overland route to safety. This proved to be an unwise move as they were never seen again.

At the end of his journey, Major Powell sat in camp and penned the following passage:

Above: Two of the pine boats used in Major John Wesley Powell's second expedition through the Grand Canyon in 1872.
PHOTO COURTESY GRAND CANYON NATIONAL PARK IDENTIFICATION NUMBER 5309

"Now the danger is over; now the toil has ceased; now the gloom has disappeared; and what a vast expanse of constellations can be seen. The river rolls by us in silent majesty; the quiet of the camp is sweet; our joy is almost ecstasy. We sit till long after midnight, talking of the Grand Canyon, talking of home, but chiefly talking of the three men who left us. Are they wandering in those depths, unable to find a way out? Are they searching over the desert lands above for water? Are they nearing the settlements?"

Major Powell and the remainder of his party, who had explored 1048 miles of the Colorado River in 98 days, did not yet realize the three missing men would never be seen again. As time went by, the general consensus was that they had been killed by a band of Paiutes living in the north Canyon. No trace of their remains was ever found.

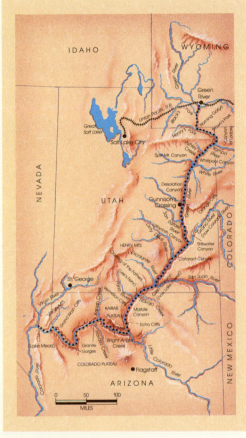

The route of Major Powell's 1869 voyage from Green River, Wyoming through the Grand Canyon to the Virgin River.

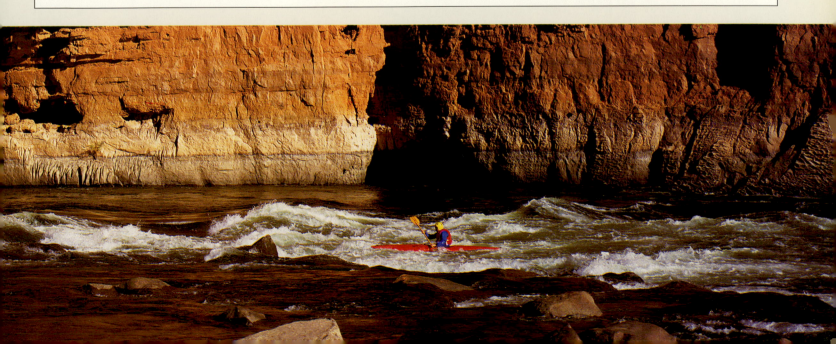

not have been able to publish his historic accounts. Far more time was spent planning the second expedition than was executed on

Above: English artist Thomas Moran sketches the Grand Canyon during John Wesley Powell's second expedition down the Colorado River.
PHOTO COURTESY GRAND CANYON NATIONAL PARK IDENTIFICATION NUMBER 5039

planning the first. Attention was focused on the exploration of both sides of the river and surveying of the Canyon was a top priority.

The accounts of both expeditions were first published in 1874. These accounts soon gained a wide readership in the United States and, after translation into several foreign languages, throughout Europe.

Major Powell's was the first of many exciting river trips by adventurers from around the world. These trips continue in record numbers today. The official report of the Powell expedition, entitled "The Exploration of the Colorado River of the West," included 29 illustrations by the famed English artist Thomas Moran and

was published by the United States Government Printing office.

President Theodore Roosevelt created the Grand Canyon National Monument in 1908.
COURTESY NATIONAL ARCHIVES

Clarence Edward Dutton, a protege of John Wesley Powell, led the first full scale geological expedition of the Grand Canyon in 1880. Dutton conducted in-depth studies of the Canyon, and its tributaries, and wrote the first volume on the geology of the Grand Canyon.

Clarence Dutton's book contained illustrations by Thomas Moran, who had illustrated the area while serving as an artist on the second expedition of Major Powell. Moran had not been a member of the river boating segment of the expedition down the canyon and had to create his drawings from photographs taken by the expedition's photographer.

Dutton, along with Major Powell, concluded that the Colorado River was older than the landforms it flowed through. They felt, erroneously, that prior to the formation of the Grand Canyon the river had cut its way deeper and deeper through the rock formations, entrenching itself as time slowly flowed by.

Throughout the late 1880s, interest in the Grand Canyon region continued to build. In 1882, Senator Benjamin Harrison introduced a bill designed to establish the Grand Canyon as a national park. The bill failed to pass on the senate floor and he reintroduced the bill again in 1883. Once again the bill failed to pass. Harrison did not give up hope and repeated the process in 1886, only to be defeated for a third time. Finally, in 1893, four years after Senator Harrison was elected as President of the United States, the Canyon was designated as the Grand

Ellsworth and Emory Kolb exploring the Grand Canyon with cameras in 1903.
PHOTO COURTESY NORTHERN ARIZONA UNIVERSITY LIBRARY

Canyon Forest Reserve through his actions, which prevented the area from seizure by prospectors and settlers and enabled the Grand Canyon to be preserved as a national treasure for all time.

Far right: Rainbow over Cedar Ridge. Rainbows appear when raindrops, mist or spray refract or reflect the sun's rays.
PHOTO BY JEFF GNASS

JOHN D. LEE AND THE MOUNTAIN MEADOWS MASSACRE

Lees Ferry, founded in 1869 by John Doyle Lee, a Mormon with seventeen wives, was a quiet town that offered the only feasible place to cross the Colorado River in this northern region of Arizona. The town's remote location provided a tranquil setting until 1877, when the heinous crimes of its founder's past rocked the small community to its foundation.

During the 1850s, Utah's Mormon population had a reputation throughout much of the rest of the country for zealotry and fanaticism. Tempers often ran high between Mormons and non-Mormons, with the exception of the local Indians, who were the Mormons only allies. Under the leadership of Brigham Young, the Mormons lived in relative peace with their Indian neighbors. They believed the Indians were brothers– "through the loins of Joseph and Manassah"– who had fallen from grace. This, the Mormons felt, was evidenced by their dark skin. The alliance between Mormons and Indians laid the groundwork for the nefarious incident that became known as the Mountain Meadows Massacre.

In 1857, the Fancher Party, emigrants from Arkansas and Missouri, drove their wagon train and 300 head of cattle through southern Utah bound for California. They made the tactless mistake of shouting insults at the Mormons and naming one of their oxen Brigham Young. One member of the wagon train boasted that the pistol he carried was the one used to kill the Mormon's martyred leader, Joseph Smith.

During this same time, the Mormons were already incensed upon learning that federal troops, under the direction of President James A. Buchanan, were en route to Utah from the east. The emigrants, prodded in part by a group of rowdy Missourians in their party, made the fatal mistake of threatening to return with an armed force once they reached California. This proved to be an tragically unfortunate boast.

The Mormons, under the leadership of Lee, who had previously been in charge of Indian affairs in southern Utah, were still smarting from the insults and years of injustices in their previous homes in Illinois, Ohio and Missouri. Any reference to the martyrdom of Joseph Smith was more than they could bear, especially

by anyone from Missouri.

Under a white flag of truce, Lee and 54 Mormon militiamen approached the Fancher Party offering to provide safe passage through a territory rife with hostile Indians. As soon as the emigrants had accepted the Mormon offer and laid down their weapons, the militiamen opened fire upon

John Doyle Lee, founder of Lees Ferry, was the only person brought to trial for the Mountain Meadows Massacre.
COURTESY ARIZONA HISTORICAL SOCIETY

the men, cutting them down where they stood. The Indians, who were allies of the Mormons, stormed the wagon train and slaughtered the women and all of the older children. When the bloodbath ended, only seventeen children, all too young to recount the incident, were alive.

For the next 20 years the community closed ranks and refused to assist the federal government in prosecuting the guilty parties. Lee fled the area and settled in the remote region that became Lees Ferry. Feeling secure in his isolation, he built the original ferry in 1872. He was only able to operate his enterprise, which continued until the Navajo Bridge was built in 1929, for a short period.

In 1875, Lee was arrested and tried for his part in the Mountain Meadows Massacre. His first trial resulted in a hung jury and he was sentenced to a lifetime in prison. After serving two years of his sentence, he was granted a new trial and released for a few months on bail. In 1877, he was again tried for his part in the massacre, the only Mormon ever tried for the grisly incident, and was convicted.

Lee accompanied his captors to Mountain Meadows where, as he sat blindfolded on the coffin that was to hold his remains, he was executed by firing squad.

EARLY DEVELOPMENT OF THE GRAND CANYON

In 1884, William Wallace Bass established a camp 27 miles west of the present site of Grand Canyon Village, near Havasupai Point. His only competition for tourist accommodations was the Farlee Hotel, a one-room shanty, that opened the same year at the junction of Peach Springs Canyon and Diamond Creek.

In 1886, John Hance, the first white settler on the South Rim, offered lodging at his ranch near Grandview Point. Hance was a colorful character and continued to offer his services as guide and tour operator at the Canyon until his death in 1919. Known to tell tall tales, Hance once said, when asked about the missing tip of one of his fingers, that he had worn

Above: Bright Angel Hotel in Grand Canyon Village was completed in 1897.
PHOTO COURTESY GRAND CANYON NATIONAL PARK IDENTIFICATION NUMBER 3494

it off pointing at the Grand Canyon.

In 1896, J. Wilbur Thurber purchased John Hance's hotel and in the following year began construction on the Bright Angel Hotel in Grand Canyon Village. Hance became the first postmaster in the Canyon, which was then called "Tourist, Arizona." In 1897, the Grand View Hotel opened its doors on the South Rim and became the first hotel to be located on the Canyon's rim.

Transportation to the Canyon took on new dimensions as the 20th century unfurled. In 1901, the first scheduled passenger train arrived. The Bright Angel Hotel was purchased by Martin Buggeln the same year.

In 1902, the first automobiles arrived and the tourist boom was on. Emory and Ellsworth Kolb established a photography studio at Grand Canyon Village in 1903 and Ralph H. Cameron, later to become a United States Senator, opened the Cameron Hotel. The same year, President Theodore Roosevelt visited the Canyon and was enamored by its beauty. President Roosevelt proclaimed the Grand Canyon a National Monument in 1908.

In 1904, the El Tovar Hotel was built by the Fred Harvey Company, who in 1906 bought the Bright Angel Hotel from Martin Buggeln.

William Wallace Bass opened the first school at the Canyon in 1911 and the following year Arizona became the nation's 48th state.

In 1914, Hermit's Rest was designed by Fred Harvey architect Mary Elizabeth Jane Colter.

The Grand View Hotel, opened in 1897, was the first hotel located on the Canyon's rim.
PHOTO COURTESY GRAND CANYON NATIONAL PARK IDENTIFICATION NUMBER 990

On February 26, 1919, Congress passed a bill, signed by President Woodrow Wilson, that established Grand Canyon National Park. The park was a territory 56 miles wide. In 1927, Grand Canyon National Park was enlarged to about 1100 square miles. A new Grand Canyon National Monument was created by President Herbert Hoover on December 22, 1932, for lands bordering the west of the national park. The 50 mile-long Marble Canyon National Monument was established on January, 20, 1969 by a bill signed by President Lyndon Johnson. The area was further enlarged by the creation of a new Grand Canyon National Park, combining the Marble Canyon, Grand Canyon National Monument and portions of the Glen Canyon and Lake Mead national recreation areas. Approximately 83,000 acres of these combined lands were deleted to enlarge the Havasupai Indian Reservation. The end result was a Grand Canyon National Park comprising 1,218,375 acres, or 1900 square miles.

Protection of the Grand Canyon was made possible by the groundwork laid by far-sighted men. Continued protection of this natural wonder is the responsibility of all who follow. When visiting the canyon, take all possible measures to keep from polluting the environment, disturbing flora or fauna, or defacing buildings or rock formations.

Today, millions of visitors from around the world visit the Grand Canyon each year, a far cry from the hundreds of years early explorers found it of little or no value.

EARLY INHABITANTS OF THE GRAND CANYON

The first residents of the Grand Canyon arrived from Asia, via the ancient land bridge across the Bering Strait, at least 11,000 years ago. These early inhabitants, Paleo-Indians called the Elephant Hunters, were nomadic tribes who found the region more tropical than it is today.

Existence of the Elephant Hunters depended mainly on hunting large prehistoric mammals; mammoth, mastodons, and elephants. Using teamwork to kill their prey, Elephant Hunters used stone spearheads with detachable foreshafts to hunt. When the main shaft was detached as their large prey struggled with their wounds, the embedded stone points would still remain and cause further damage to the animal.

Approximately 7500 years ago, the Elephant Hunters evolved into a more advanced culture known as the Archaics. These early Native Americans were still hunters, even though

Approximately 1500 years ago the Anasazi arrived at the eastern Grand Canyon and the Cohonina entered the western regions of the Canyon. More than 2000 Anasazi sites have been discovered including Tusayan Pueblo, about three miles west of Desert View on the South Rim. Tusayan Pueblo was constructed around 1185 AD and housed between 25 and 30 people in a community environment.

The Anasazi were hunter-gatherers who also cultivated crops of corn, squash and beans. Peaceful people, they traded with their western neighbors, the Cohonina, who were also farmers. For reasons still unknown, the Anasazi, whose name means "the ancient ones," and

the Cohonina abandoned their Grand Canyon homes about 800 years ago. It is generally believed the Anasazi traveled eastward and became the ancestors of, or merged with, the Hopi who are still pueblo dwellers and are present in northern Arizona today.

The next residents to occupy the Canyon were the Cerbats, who moved into the region about 150 years after the exodus of the Anasazi and Cohonina. The Cerbats were the ancestors of the Havasupai and Hulapai who today occupy two separate reservations in the western Grand Canyon.

Around the same time as the arrival of the Cerbats, the Southern Paiutes began to appear

Above: Indian artists produced drawings, called pictographs, with paint colors made from rock and plants.   PHOTO BY JERRY JACKA

their game was smaller, more modern, species than the prehistoric beasts their ancestors had hunted. The earliest human artifacts to be discovered in the Grand Canyon region were split-twig animal figurines fashioned from single green willow twigs. It is thought that these figurines were used by the Archaics as fetishes to ensure magical powers while hunting. The Archaics inhabited the region until approximately 3000 years ago.

There exists a gap in the record from the point of the departure of the Archaic and the arrival of the Anasazi and Cohonina about 1500 years later. It appears that no humans occupied the Grand Canyon during this period for reasons that are yet unknown.

Right: Anasazi granaries at Nankoweap ruin. Built into the Canyon's wall, 500 feet above the Colorado River, these granaries were used by the Anasazi to store their crops.
PHOTO BY TOM TILL

on the Canyon's North Rim. The Southern Paiutes, who still today occupy lands north of the Grand Canyon, were commonly thought to have been responsible for the killing of three members of Major John Wesley Powell's historic river expedition of 1869. The three expedition members left the Powell group to find a safer route overland after experiencing more adventure in the white-water rapids of the Canyon than they had bargained for. After leaving the main party, these unfortunate adventurers were never heard from again.

Left: Petroglyphs were made by scratching or carving designs into rock surfaces.
PHOTO BY GARY LADD

The last group of Native Americans to arrive in the Grand Canyon area were the Navajo, who entered the region approximately 600 years ago. The Navajo were Athabascans whose origins have been traced to Canada. They are thought to have migrated to the Southwest around 1000 years ago. They lived a peaceful existence in the region for hundreds of years, trading with their pueblo dwelling neighbors, until their conflicts with the white man in the early 1800's. Strongly independent people, the Navajo suffered greatly at the hands of the white man in grossly one-sided conflicts. The Navajo Reservation now borders the eastern side of the Grand Canyon.

WILDLIFE

In all the world, few areas have a greater variety of wildlife than the Grand Canyon. More than 287 species of birds frequent the area, along with 88 species of mammals, 50 species of reptiles and 8 different species of amphibians calling the Canyon home. This broad assortment of fauna is evident mainly because of one special factor– altitude. With elevations ranging from 1200 feet above sea level at the western end of the Canyon to 9100 feet on the North Rim, the Grand Canyon includes four of the seven life zones found on the North American continent, which provide habitats for broad displays of flora and fauna. More than 60 percent of all species of wildlife found in North America are present in Arizona, with most in evidence in the Grand Canyon area.

The Grand Canyon's diversity of plant life, including more than 1000 different flowering plants, provides food and shelter for the park's animal populations. Six species of large mammals reside within the park's boundaries, and can be found in various life zones including elk, *Cervus canadensis*, mule deer, *Odocoileus hemionus,* mountain lion, *Felis concolor,* black bear, *Ursus americanus,* bighorn sheep, *Ovis canadensis,* and pronghorn, *Antilocarpa americana.* The largest of these species is the elk, which is also known as wapiti.

The present elk species, the Rocky Mountain elk, was transplanted in several stages to the region from Yellowstone National Park in the years between 1913 and 1928. The original elk the first white settlers encountered in the region were Merriam elk, which disappeared around the turn of the century. The reasons for the complete disappearance of this species are still unclear. It is unlikely that the small number of hunters present at that time could have killed the Merriam elk down to the last animal. It is more probable that competition by grazing livestock, or diseases introduced by domestic herds, may have been the more significant factors.

Pronghorn antelope are not really antelope, despite their name, and are closer relatives of the mountain goat than the true antelope. The pronghorn is the only member of the family *Antilocapridae,* and is only found in North America. Pronghorn are capable of running at speeds greater than 60 miles per hour. The only faster animal is the Asiatic or African cheetah. This great speed, coupled with widespread eyes giving the pronghorn 180 degree vision, enables the pronghorn to elude most of its natural enemies.

Mule deer are the most widely distributed game animals in Arizona and are found in the various life zones of the Grand Canyon and throughout the state. During the 1950s and early 1960s, the mule deer population became so large that starvation was imminent. Nature took its toll following a particularly severe winter in 1954-1955 and nearly 20,000 mule deer starved. Today, the Arizona Game and Fish Department keeps close tabs on mule

Raccoon, *Procyon lotor,* although not as common in the Canyon area as their close relative the ringtail, *Bassariscus astutus,* are one of nature's most handsome mammals. These nocturnal animals are found in riparian communities and are omnivorous, eating both plants and small animals.

Left: A young mule deer, *Odocoileus hemionus,* in velvet. Each year mule deer bucks shed their antlers, growing a new pair each spring.
PHOTO BY JAMES TALLON

Right: Bobcats, *Lynx rufus,* are fairly common residents of the Grand Canyon. Adults normally weigh between 18 and 25 pounds although it is not uncommon for males to reach 30 pounds.
PHOTO BY LEONARD LEE RUE III

deer populations throughout the state.

Of a more dangerous note, the Canyon once had two species of bear; black bear and grizzly bear, *Ursus horribilis.* It is commonly thought that the last grizzly in Arizona was killed in the White Mountains in 1916. The black bear is still sighted in more mountainous regions of the Canyon.

Another predator of note is the mountain lion, also known as cougar, panther, painter or catamount. The mountain lion, a member of the cat family, often reaches a length of four feet and can weigh more than 125 pounds. Roaming through a wide range of habitats, these large cats prey on elk, deer and even domestic livestock.

Bighorn sheep can be found in the Piñon-Juniper Woodland communities and in Desert Scrub communities in the Grand Canyon area. Although bighorn populations have been greatly reduced throughout much of their range in the last century, at one time they were more plentiful than elk and deer, sporting large enough numbers to serve as the primary meat source for many Native American groups found in the region. Although excessive hunting greatly reduced the bighorn populations, the introduction of domestic livestock is also thought to have played an important role in their decline. Domestic sheep introduced disease to native bighorn populations and the grazing of both sheep and cattle in their range caused a shortage of food for the bighorn.

Bighorn, normally reclusive, are known for their ability to climb steep slopes and can negotiate even the most difficult terrain with an ease found in few other animals.

Among the smaller mammals found in the Grand Canyon area are the badger, *Taxidea taxus,* gray fox, *Urocyon cinereoargenteus,* bobcat, *Lynx rufus,* coyote, *Canis latrans,* porcupine, *Erethizon dorsatum,* raccoon, *Procyon lotor,* ringtail, *Bassariscus astutus,* along with a variety of squirrel, rabbit and other rodents. Beaver, *Castor canadensis,* may still be found along the streams.

More than 287 bird species may be found, the smallest of which is the hummingbird and the largest is the Merriam wild turkey. Also seen are quail, dove, turkey vultures, red-tailed hawks, roadrunner, owls, woodpecker, purple martin, raven, cactus wren and more.

Above: An alert mule deer doe in the Spruce-Fir Forest of the Grand Canyon's North Rim.
PHOTO BY JAMES TALLON

Left: Black bear is the only bear species to still be found in the Grand Canyon region. Although classified as carnivores, black bear also feed on roots and berries.
PHOTO BY JAMES TALLON

1. Deer mouse
2. Gopher snake
3. Kaibab squirrel
4. Wild turkey
5. Western bluebird
6. Mule deer
7. Porcupine
8. Northern plateau lizard
9. Steller's jay
10. Bobcat
11. Common flicker

A. Blue elderberry
B. Ponderosa pine
C. Gambel oak
D. Mountain Mahogany

Above: Rocky Mountain elk, *Cervus canadensis,* were transplanted from Yellowstone National Park to Grand Canyon National Park in several stages between 1913 and 1928.
PHOTO BY JAMES TALLON

The Yellow-Pine Woodland Community is found between 7000 and 8200 foot elevations and are characterized by ponderosa (yellow) pine, *Pinus ponderosa,* Gambel oak, *Quercus gambelii,* blue elderberry, *Sambucus cerulea,* and mountain mahogany, *Cerocarpus ledifolius*. Yellow-Pine Woodlands are generally more open than those at higher elevations, allowing grasses and shrubs to grow on the forest floor. Rainfall is normally in excess of 20 inches annually. This mountain community is home to mule deer, bobcat, porcupine and the Kaibab squirrel.

The Kaibab squirrel is found only at the North Rim of the Grand Canyon. This large, white-tailed squirrel is distinctive for its ear tufts, or tassels. The Kaibab closely resembles the Aberts squirrel, which also has tufted ears.

Above: The red-tailed hawk, *Buteo jamaicensis,* is the most common large hawk found in the Grand Canyon region.
PHOTO BY JAMES TALLON

Thousands of years ago, the Grand Canyon separated the Kaibab and the Aberts squirrels and through the ensuing years the Kaibab developed totally white tails while the Aberts' tails are black on top and white beneath.

Kaibab squirrels build their nests high in the ponderosa pine and feed on the inner bark and pine seeds of the tree. In summer they occasionally feed on mushrooms.

Yellow-Pine Woodlands are also home to the Merriam turkey, the largest of Arizona's bird species. They may sometimes drop down to Piñon-Juniper Woodlands in times of heavy snow, although they prefer to remain in the tall pines for their roost sites. They are polygamous. Males round up a harem of females and remain with them throughout mating season. Physiological changes occur causing the male's head to turn deep red or purple. When the mating urge strikes, he puffs up to nearly twice his normal size and struts, with his tail fanned like a peacock, about the forest hoping to attract the attention of a female.

SPRUCE-FIR AND MOUNTAIN GRASSLAND COMMUNITIES

Generally restricted to elevations above 8200 feet, the Spruce-Fir Forest consists of a mix of blue spruce, *Picea pungens,* aspen, *Populus tremuloides,* white fir, *Abies concolor,* Douglas fir, *Pseudotsuga menziesii,* and Englemann spruce, *Picea engelmannii.* This community's high altitude creates a short growing season of about three months and cold winters with heavy snowfalls.

The canopy of the forest so dense that few shrubs and grasses exist except in meadows scattered throughout the forest. Biologists call this the Mountain Grassland Community.

The Spruce-Fir Forest is home to a wide variety of fauna. Rocky Mountain mule deer can be seen in early morning or just before sundown. Squirrels scamper about throughout the day along with chipmunks and a great assortment of birds. In the evenings, bobcats search for their prey.

The Spruce-Fir and Mountain Grassland communities are also home to the porcupine. Although sometimes a meal for a bobcat or mountain lion, porcupine rarely run, or hide, from danger. At the first hint of approaching predators, thousands of needle-sharp quills spring to attention, making the porcupine a less-than-attractive meal for all but the most foolhardy diner. Porcupine grow to more than two feet in the body with tails that can be up to 14 inches long, all one big pincushion!

SCREECH OWL

Owls are normally nocturnal birds of prey and feed primarily on rodents and small animals. These large-headed, short-necked, birds can best be seen at dusk or after dark. The large eyes of the owl are fixed in their sockets, forcing them to move their entire head in order to shift their gaze.

Extremely quiet hunters, the owl flies silently through the darkness, catching their prey completely off guard. Most owls are cavity nesters but will occupy structures built by man on occasion. The female owl is normally larger than the male and immature owls closely resemble adults.

The Grand Canyon is home to several species of owl, including great horned owl, *Bubo virginianus,* flammulated owl, *Otus flammeolus,* long eared owl, *Asio otus,* burrowing owl, *Athene cunicularia,* northern pygmy owl, *Glaucidium gnoma,* spotted owl, *Strix occidentalis,* northern saw-whet owl, *Aegolius acadicus,* and common screech owl, *Otus kennicottii.* Owls may be found throughout any of the biotic communities of the Grand Canyon.

Left: The common screech owl's flat facial disk contains large external ear flaps. Their erect ear tufts give them a questioning look.
PHOTO BY LEONARD LEE RUE III

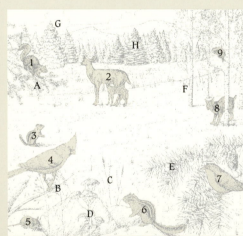

1. Red squirrel
2. Mule deer and fawn
3. Golden-mantled ground squirrel
4. Steller's jay
5. Deer mouse
6. Uinta chipmunk
7. Western bluebird
8. Bobcat
9. Porcupine

A. Douglas fir
B. Kentucky bluegrass
C. Letterman needlegrass
D. Yarrow
E. Engelmann spruce
F. Aspen
G. White fir
H. Blue spruce

Sometimes referred to as the pygmy forest because of the small stature of its trees, the Piñon-Juniper Woodland Community can be found in elevations of the Transition life zone, between 3500 and 7000 foot elevations. This community occurs in the Benchlands and on both rims of the Grand Canyon. Dominated by piñon pine, *Pinus cembrioides,* and one-seed juniper, *Juniperus monosperma,* Piñon-Juniper Woodland usually shows patches of chaparral species in more open areas.

Both chaparral and woodlands are intermediate areas between desert and forest in terms of moisture, elevation and temperature. The chaparral is dominant in more arid and rocky soils, while woodlands prefer finer soils and slightly more moisture. In some areas, Arizona oak, *Quercus arizonica,* Gambel oak, *Quercus gambelli,* Gray oak, *Quercus grisea,* and Emory oak *Quercus emoryi,* may be found along with Mormon tea cliffrose, *Ephedra viridis,* rabbit bush, *Chrysothamnus viscidiflorus,* and banana yucca, *Yucca baccata.*

The Piñon-Juniper Woodland Community is home to a wide variety of animal life. Desert bighorn, in danger of extinction in many areas, may be found in the more isolated regions of this community. Mountain lion, the largest of Arizona predators, is active mainly at night but may sometimes be seen traveling its wide range during daylight hours. Mule deer are often seen at dawn and dusk.

Below: Desert bighorn, exterminated in much of their former range by hunting, disease and competition for browse with livestock, are currently seen in a few isolated areas. PHOTO BY JAMES TALLON

1. Sonoran gopher snake
2. Cliff chipmunk
3. Short-horned lizard
4. Desert cottontail
5. Southern plateau lizard
6. Yellow-backed spiny lizard
7. Gray fox
8. Desert bighorn
9. Mule deer
10. Mountain lion
11. Raven
12. Downy woodpecker

A. Utah juniper
B. Mormon tea
C. Cliffrose
D. Rabbit bush
E. Gambel oak
F. Piñon pine
G. Banana yucca

RIPARIAN COMMUNITY

The Riparian Community occurs along the banks of continually moist streams, lakes, and rivers. These streamside biotic communities may exist along perennial or intermittent bodies of water as long as the banks remain moist enough to sustain flora and fauna relying on the area for nourishment. In the Grand Canyon, riparian communities are a stark contrast to drier biotic communities surrounding them, oases in an otherwise arid area.

The densest vegetation occurs in the Riparian Community. Here box elder, *Acer negundo,* seep willow, *Baccharis glutinosa,* sycamore, *Platanus wrightii,* and Goodding willow, *Salix gooddingii,* share the banks with monkeyflower, *Diplacus aurantiacus,* watercress and maidenhair fern. Other flora species from neighboring communities are also present in riparian areas allowing great diversity from one Riparian Community to another.

Riparian communities are important to most animals found in the Riparian Community and in other communities. Deer, elk and coyote enter riparian areas each evening for water. Certain species, including raccoons, skunks, ringtail, beaver and gray fox are most common in riparian communities. Other species live only in riparian areas including salamanders, toads and garter snakes.

Although most species of birds rely on the Riparian Community for water, the mourning dove, hairy woodpecker, western kingbird, belted kingfisher and others are largely limited to the Riparian Community for nesting.

In addition to providing an environment for fish and amphibians, the Riparian Community is also home to numerous algae, fungi and insects that are vital links in the food chain feeding the higher members of the various biotic communities found in the region.

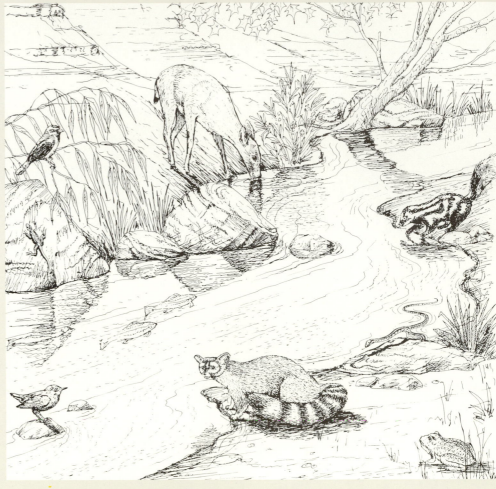

Above: The great blue heron nest singly, or in colonies, along the banks of streams and rivers.
PHOTO BY JAMES TALLON

Below: Beavers can be found in the Riparian Community building dams of branches, leaves and twigs, which they also eat.
PHOTO BY LEONARD LEE RUE III

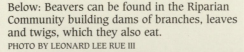

1. American dipper
2. Rainbow trout
3. Black-throated sparrow
4. Northern whiptail lizard
5. Mule deer
6. Ringtail
7. Wandering garter snake
8. Rocky Mountain toad
9. Spotted skunk

A. Goodding willow
B. Arrowweed
C. Seep-willow
D. Arizona sycamore

Existing primarily in areas less than 4500 feet in elevation, the Desert Scrub Community is characterized by widely-spaced, drought resistant plants. The Benchlands of the Tonto Plateau, the Esplanade and Inner Canyon areas away from streams and rivers all contain Desert Scrub communities. Desert Scrub is home to a wide variety of flora and fauna that are able to exist in arid and semi-arid conditions.

Desert Scrub supports a variety of cacti and small-leaved bushes, each capable of sustaining life during periods of drought. The cacti, including several species of agave and yucca, ocotillo, *Fouquieria splendens,* barrel cactus, *Ferocactus wislizenii,* several cholla species, organ pipe cactus, *Cereus thurberi,* prickly pear cactus, *Opuntia phaeacantha* and beavertail, *Opuntia basilaris.* The most predominant plant is the blackbush, *Coleogyne ramosissima,* with its woody stems and small leaves.

Fauna of this community are hearty breeds. Coyote, bighorn and jackrabbit share these regions with Grand Canyon rattlesnake, desert striped whipsnake, California kingsnake and collared lizards. A lack of trees causes most birds to nest in other areas and use Desert Scrub only to forage. A few species, including Gambel quail, *Callipepla gambelii,* and road-runner, *Geococcyx californianus,* nest either on the ground or in low bushes.

Below: Coyotes, *canis latrans,* are members of the *canidae* family and can be found in all areas of the Canyon. In the evening you may hear packs howling.   PHOTO BY JAMES TALLON

1. Grand Canyon rattlesnake
2. Chuckwalla
3. Harris ground squirrel
4. Roadrunner
5. Desert bighorn
6. Coyote
7. Jackrabbit
8. Cactus wren

A. Yucca
B. Ocotillo
C. Prickly pear cactus
D. Barrel cactus
E. Teddy bear cholla
F. Four-wing saltbush
G. Organ pipe cactus
H. Century plant
I. Jumping cholla

FLORA

Flora of the Grand Canyon exists in six biotic communities dispersed through four life zones. In the study of ecology, a science dealing with all living things, seven life zones were established between the equator and the North Pole in a study of flora and fauna formulated during the late nineteenth century by Clinton Hart Merriam for the United States Department of Agriculture. Merriam's study was based on the premise that a change of 1000 feet in elevation will have the same effect on plant life as changes of 300 to 500 miles in latitude. He also determined temperature drops 3.5 to 5 degrees for each 1000 foot rise in elevation.

The Spruce-Fir and Mountain Grassland Community, generally restricted to elevations above 8200 feet, contain mixtures of aspen, blue spruce, white fir, Engelmann spruce and Douglas fir. The Yellow-Pine Woodland Community, found between 7000 and 8200 foot elevations, is comprised of ponderosa pine, Gambel oak, blue elderberry and mountain mahogany. The Piñon-Juniper Woodland Community, which is found in elevations of the Transition Life Zone, between 3500 and 7000 foot elevations, is dominated by piñon pine and one-seed juniper.

The Desert Scrub Community, which exists primarily in areas less than 4500 feet, is home to numerous cacti and drought resistant plants. The Riparian Community found along rivers and streams provides important habitat and much needed moisture for many of the Canyon's flora and fauna species.

The extreme variances in altitude along the Canyon walls allows wide variety in natural vegetation to occur within a relatively small area. Sometimes separated by a very narrow horizontal space on maps, but by hundreds of foot difference in altitude, several biotic communities may occur.

North Rim and South Rim vegetation are vastly different. Viewing one from the other can be deceptive in trying to comprehend the difference in altitude. From the South Rim, the North Rim appears forested and from the North Rim the South Rim appears sparsely vegetated in most areas.

The South Rim supports an open steppe which is dominated by piñon pine and Utah juniper with a sparse understory of shrubs and grasses. There are few blossoming plants and those present have relatively short flowering seasons. The soil is red, sandy, or of clay, and is thin in most places.

The North Rim, on the Kaibab Plateau, has a much higher altitude and its vegetation is typically of a more mountainous nature, with its highest points covered by forest and grassy meadows. Because of severe over-grazing by deer between 1906 and 1924, much of the original understory was removed and has not yet recovered. In place of the original plants are thickets of shrubs, including pink locust, which is of little interest to grazing animals.

Agave, *Agave havardi,* also called mescal, was used for a wide variety of purposes by Native Americans including as a food source and as a source of fiber. Agave is widespread throughout the Canyon, preferring open, rocky places. Called century plants from misconceptions regarding flowering, agave actually bloom once, after a period of 15-25 years, when they send a tall, stick-like stalk towering into the air above the plant. Once the plant flowers it begins to die.

Preceding Pages: Scarlet monkeyflower, *Mimulus cardinalis,* and box elder, *Acer negundo,* along Havasu Creek in Havasu Canyon.
PHOTO BY LARRY ULRICH

Left: Aspen, *Populus tremuloides,* on the North Rim begin to change color in the early fall. The North Rim is home to Spruce-Fir and Mountain Grassland communities, which are generally found in elevations above 8200 feet.
PHOTO BY MICHAEL FATALI

Right: Scarlet monkeyflower and watercress, *Nasturtium officinale,* grow in precarious niches along Tapeats Creek.
PHOTO BY LARRY ULRICH

Flora Continued...

Vegetation on the Canyon walls is comprised of shrubs and herbs which are able to germinate and cling to the rapidly eroding features. Scrub oak, mountain mahogany, and cliffrose form thickets on the steep walls, while small stands of Douglas fir and bigtooth maple fill recesses in the cooler sites.

Vegetation at the Grand Canyon's floor is determined by the water's flow and geological formations of the Canyon's walls. Sides of the Canyon that are constantly eroded by running water form smooth rock walls where plants have trouble gaining a foothold. Walls are occasionally streaked by flowlines of lichens that follow the flow of moisture down the wall's surface. Along the water's edge, and on some sandbars, stands of willows, cottonwood, tamarisk and weedy herbs, including seep-willow, wild licorice and cocklebur occur.

In a region with altitude changes that are as extreme as those found in the Grand Canyon, it is possible for species of plants to survive by making short migrations, up or down the Canyon walls, as the climate changes. The Grand Canyon contains elements of all flora that has inhabited it since its first ability to colonize land plants.

The Sonoran element enters the Canyon at its westernmost points, and only a small group of representative plants, such as the creosote bush, Ocotillo, yucca, prickly pear, cholla, barrel cactus, agave and organ pipe cactus actually reach the borders of the national park.

With a wide variety of natural habitats, and a difference in elevation of nearly 8000 feet from the North Rim to the lowest points on the Canyon floor, the Canyon contains more than 1400 species of plants.

Flora of the Canyon includes rare "hanging gardens," formed on moist ledges watered by spray from waterfalls, or water seeping from springs or through cracks in the rocks. These hanging gardens contain wild flowers, annuals, and biennials predominantly belonging to the mustard, phlox, knotweed, borage and daisy families; and perennials, which blossom soon after the final snow melt. All species depend on winter rains and snows to produce rich assemblages in the early spring.

The late spring and early summer finds the Canyon alive with the flowering of shrubby plants including bitterbush, cliffrose, and fernbush. In late summer, sagebrush and rabbitbush blossoms are visible in large displays.

From the first blooms of spring through the summer's second flowering season the Grand Canyon puts on a continual show of color in its various biotic communities.

Right: Claretcup, *Echinocereus triglochidatus*, may often be seen blossoming in May and June on both rims of the Canyon. It blooms as early as April at lower elevations of the Inner Canyon.
PHOTO BY JERRY JACKA

Below: Desert marigold, *Baileya multiradiata*, in bloom at the base of Lava Falls.
PHOTO BY LARRY ULRICH

FLORA CONTINUED...

Below: Indian paintbrush is known for the bright red of its flowers. The two most common species are wholeleaf paintbrush, *Castilleja integra,* and narrow-leaved paintbrush, *Castilleja linariaefolia.* The wholeleaf variety is most common and is found in dry, sunny places on the South Rim. The narrow-leaved paintbrush is found on both rims and also is seen in the Inner Canyon.
PHOTO BY JERRY SIEVE

Above: The most common summer and fall flowering aster on the South Rim, the hoary aster, *Aster foliaceus,* is a member of the sunflower family. Asters are biennial, or perennial, and are common throughout most of the life zones of the Canyon. This plant is being pollinated by a Painted Lady butterfly.
PHOTO BY JAMES TALLON

Above: Engelmann's prickly pear, *Opuntia engelmannii,* is a wide spreading cactus that reaches up to 15 feet in diameter. Prickly pear fruit, called tunas, are used to make jelly and dye and are eaten by birds and rodents. Stems are used in face creams and to purify water.
PHOTO BY STEVE BRUNO

Above: Several species of evening primrose are evident in the Canyon area. Evening primrose opens their flowers in the evening after the heat of the day has passed. Each flower has a life span of one day and dies as morning sunlight hits. Because evening primrose only flower at night, night-flying insects pollinate them after being drawn to the flower by its fragrance. Night flowering allows the plant to retain its moisture and flower throughout the hottest months.
PHOTO BY DICK DIETRICH

Above: Barrel cactus, *Ferocactus wislizenii*, may grow to heights of more than ten feet with a diameter of as much as two feet, although they are generally much smaller. Barrel cactus are not filled with water, but are filled with a slimy alkaline juice. Its hooked spines were used as fishhooks by Native Americans who also ate the fruit. Barrel cactus bloom in many colors in the Grand Canyon region. Here, a bee pollinates the flower in the lower right corner.
PHOTO BY JERRY JACKA

Right: Scarlet monkeyflower, *Mimulus cardinalis,* and maidenhair fern, *Asplenium trichomanes,* in a "hanging garden." The Inner Canyon is noted for its rare hanging gardens, created as moisture from the spray of waterfalls, or by water seeping from springs through cracks in the rock, nurtures plants growing on ledges on the Canyon walls. Hanging gardens, appearing to grow out of the sides of the Canyon walls, are oases and feature endemic species such as the primrose *Primula hunnewellii,* with its beautiful pink flowers and sedge, *Eriophorum chamissonis*.
PHOTO BY LARRY ULRICH

THE SOUTH RIM

Desert bighorn, *Ovis canadensis*, have been exterminated in much of their former range. Currently, they are found only in a few isolated areas of Piñon-Juniper Woodland and Desert Scrub communities.

The South Rim, home to almost all of the Grand Canyon's visitor facilities, is open for visitation year round. In addition to being the most visited, and developed, area of the Grand Canyon, the South Rim is also the center of most activities in the region. From Grand Canyon Village, the site of the majority of visitor accommodations, two roads lead along the South Rim; East Rim Drive and West Rim Drive.

East Rim Drive runs twenty-one miles east to the park's eastern entrance and to Desert View. Although accommodations are limited, they include a general store, souvenir shop, gasoline station and campground. Three miles to the west of Desert View are Tusayan Ruins, built by the Anasazi in approximately 1185 AD, and a museum. East Rim Drive's route is primarily through Ponderosa Pine Woodland, with mature trees reaching heights of 125 feet.

East Rim Drive also leads to the head of the South Kaibab Trail, near Yaki Point, which is almost 21 miles in length. The trail, actually two hiking trails that lead from the North Rim to the South Rim, leads up and down steep trails and passes through four life zones.

West Rim Drive begins at the western end of Grand Canyon Village and continues eight miles to Hermit's Rest. Many of the better known landmarks of the South Rim are to be found along West Rim Drive, including Maricopa Point, Hopi Point and Pima Point. Elevations along West Rim Drive are lower than those along East Rim Drive. Altitudes at the South Rim, between 6000 and 7500 feet, are generally about 1500 feet lower than those at the North Rim. Grand Canyon Village, at 6860 feet above sea level, is approximately mid-range for South Rim elevations.

West Rim Drive's route is primarily through Piñon-Juniper Woodland, featuring short one-seed juniper and piñon pine evergreens that seldom reach more than 25 feet in height and form open, sparsely vegetated areas.

Average annual precipitation at the South Rim is 14.46 inches, with annual snowfalls of 64.9 inches. January is the coldest month with temperatures averaging 30.5°F. The record low temperature for the South Rim was -16°F in 1949. The warmest month is July, with a mean temperature of 69.4°F. The warmest temperature ever recorded occurred in June of 1933, when the mercury soared to 98°F.

Spring brings a cacophony of wildflowers to the South Rim. Although some species may flower earlier in the Inner Canyon, South Rim flowers generally bloom about a month earlier than those at higher elevations on the North Rim. Spring flowers gradually diminish as the weather warms during the hot, dry days of June. In early July, afternoon thunderstorms bring forth a second flowering season.

South Rim visitation can only be enhanced by journeys to the Grand Canyon's North Rim and, for the more adventurous traveler, a trek to the Inner Canyon.

Left: Sunrise from Mather Point on the South Rim of the Grand Canyon.
PHOTO BY LARRY ULRICH

Right: Pima Point on the South Rim of the Grand Canyon. The South Rim is the most visited area of the Grand Canyon.
PHOTO BY LARRY ULRICH

Following pages: The South Rim on a winter morning. The South Rim receives an average of 64.9 inches of snowfall each year.
PHOTO BY JERRY SIEVE

THE NORTH RIM

The Grand Canyon's North Rim offers an entirely different perspective than that of the more frequently visited South Rim. Its remote location, coupled with heavy annual snowfalls which close the area to visitors from October through May, makes the North Rim much less accessible than the South Rim. In places the lights of the South Rim are visible, less than 11 miles away from the North Rim as the crow flies, but more than 200 miles away by automobile.

Approximately 1500 feet higher in average elevation than the South Rim, the North Rim is the Grand Canyon's coolest and wettest area. Average snowfall is 128.7 inches and rainfall reaches an average of 22.78 inches. January has a mean temperature of 28.7°F, with a record low of -25°F during February of 1957. July is the warmest month with mean temperatures of 61.7°F. The hottest temperature on record at the North Rim was in July of 1939, when the mercury topped 91°F.

The higher elevations of the North Rim, up to 9165 feet, and the resulting cool and moist environment in elevations above 8200 feet, provide the setting for dense Spruce-Fir and Mountain Grassland communities. White fir, blue spruce, Aspen, Engelmann spruce, and Douglas fir create a dense forest canopy, allowing for few shrubs and grasses on the forest floor. The wildflowers on the North Rim frequently flower later than their counterparts on the South Rim. Cold winters and heavy snowfall only allows a short growing season of about three months.

The North Rim is comprised of parts of four plateaus; the Shivwits Plateau, Unikaret Plateau, Kanab Plateau, and Kaibab Plateau. The Shivwits Plateau is the westernmost and includes Grand Wash Fault and Hurricane Fault. The Unikaret Plateau falls between Hurricane Fault and Toroweap Fault and is home to Vulcan's Throne, Toroweap Overlook, Mount Trumball and Mount Logan.

Bordered by Toroweap Fault on the west and the Kaibab Plateau on the east, the Kanab Plateau is home to Kanab Creek, which slices deep into the plateau's layers of Kaibab and Toroweap limestone. Kanab Creek is the only major tributary feeding the Colorado River from the northern plateaus.

The Kaibab Plateau is the area most visitors to the North Rim are most familiar with. The Kaibab Plateau rests between 7000 and 9000 feet above sea level and contains a forest and animal community more mountainous in nature than other plateaus of the North Rim.

Near the tip of Bright Angel Point, is The Grand Canyon Lodge, the North Rim's only lodging. Additional visitor accommodations are north of the park's entrance and at Jacob's Lake, thirty-two miles from the entrance. The more famous of North Rim landmarks include Mount Hayden, Buddha Temple, Isis Temple, Brahma Temple, Angel's Window, Tower of Ra, Shiva Temple, Wotan's Throne and Cape Royal.

Ponderosa pine, *Pinus ponderosa,* also known as yellow pine, are the predominant species of Yellow-Pine Woodland communities of the Grand Canyon. They can be found on the North Rim and in higher elevations of the South Rim. They are the most common pine found in Arizona.

Left: Fall colors in the Spruce-Fir Community of the North Rim.
PHOTO BY DICK DIETRICH

Right: Angel's Window on the North Rim, near Cape Royal, is a large natural arch framing a view of the Canyon beyond.
PHOTO BY BOB CLEMENZ

HAVASU CANYON

The Havasupai have inhabited Havasu Canyon since before the arrival of the first Europeans to the area. A peaceful, agrarian people, the Havasupai share the splendor of their canyon with a variety of flora and fauna and have always welcomed visitors with open arms.

Widely described as Paradise, Utopia and Shangri-la, the beauty of Havasu Canyon defies description by words and photographs alone. Published descriptions of this tranquil oasis in the southwestern corner of the Grand Canyon, always fall short of the splendor of this secluded destination.

Travel to Havasu Canyon can pose a bit of a challenge for the casual visitor. The route begins seven miles east of Peach Springs, at Indian Route 18, and continues across the Hulapai Indian Reservation to Supai trailhead at Hulapai hilltop. From there the journey continues on foot, down to the bottom of Hulapai Canyon and on through the gorge to Havasu Canyon and the village of Supai.

Havasu Canyon offers a stunning contrast to the barren terrain of the Canyon rim above. Nearly 3000 feet below the Canyon's rim, The canyon is a lush, semi-tropical wonderland where a wide variety of flora and fauna, along with an Indian tribe, enjoy the bounty of a streamside community. Havasu Creek flows through the canyon's gorge, its spring fed waters a striking contrast to the chocolate colored water of the Colorado River.

The creek emerges from natural springs and as its mineral laden waters begin their journey through the canyon, traveling through Redwall Limestone walls, it brings sustenance to all who call Havasu Canyon home.

As Havasu Creek travels down the canyon, plunging over precipitous cliffs and creating numerous waterfalls and cascades, minerals in the water leave deposits of travertine, creating small dams and pools. The pools, a spectacular blue-green color, provide water for the Riparian Community along the banks of Havasu Creek.

The area has been home to Native Americans for more than 1000 years. It is not certain that the current residents, the Havasupai, whose name means "the people that live where the waters are blue-green," are the original dwellers, or if they inherited their canyon home from earlier residents. The Havasupai inhabit the village of Supai, deep within the towering walls of Havasu Canyon, in what has to be the most remarkably beautiful location in all of Arizona and the Southwest.

The first written records of the Havasupai date from 1776 when Father Francisco Garces, a Spanish missionary, visited the area. For the next century, there was little contact with the Europeans, except for the determined trappers and prospectors that visited the area.

The Havasupai have always been peaceful people and enjoy occasional visitors to their remote location. Throughout the centuries their existence depended on farming the lush and fertile lands of Havasu Canyon and supplementing their diets by hunting small game. Today, their existence depends on raising livestock. Corn, squash and beans are their staples and their fruit crops consist of peaches, nectarines, apricots and figs. Peaches are said to have been introduced to the Havasupai by

Left: Mooney Falls was named for prospector James Mooney who fell to his death near the falls in 1880. At 196 feet, Mooney Falls is the highest waterfall in Havasu Canyon.
PHOTO BY LARRY ULRICH

Right: Beaver Falls is a series of cascades that include several falls in the 20–30 foot range that produce a number of large, picturesque turquoise pools.
PHOTO BY STEVE BRUNO

John D. Lee, a Mormon fugitive who lived among these people for several years following his involvement in the events surrounding Mountain Meadows Massacre.

For many centuries the Havasupai have been engaged in inter-tribal trade with their Native American neighbors. The Hulapai to the west, who share a common language with the Havasupai, trade raw deer hides in exchange for fruit and vegetables. The Navajo and Hopi trade blankets, wool and silver jewelry for dressed skins and agricultural products.

Havasupai men are responsible for tanning hides, which were in the past deer, antelope, and bighorn sheep. Today they tan primarily cattle skins and deer hides obtained from their trade with the Hulapai.

Havasupai women make baskets of two main types; larger baskets with a loose weave and small ones that are tightly woven. Large baskets are primarily made for their own use while smaller baskets, made of small willow or acacia branches, are made for sale to tourists.

Havasu Creek surfaces less than a half mile up Havasu Canyon from its junction with Hulapai Canyon. Water flow of water at the beginning of the creek is not impressive. It gradually increases in volume as it travels down the canyon and small side streams add volume to the flow. Small springs increase the rush of the creek's waters, finally gaining the appearance of being fully formed a short distance below its origin.

The force of Havasu Creek, running rapidly down the canyon through Redwall Limestone, has created several falls in Havasu Canyon. Since limestone is harder than sandstone, the force of the water has eroded the sandstone deposits at a faster rate than the limestone. This leaves shelves of limestone over which the creek rushes, creating a waterfall. For a waterfall to be considered a major fall it must have a height greater than 75 feet.

Because of the nature of water erosion, the resulting falls are slowly changing their form. The force of the creek's water, and mineral deposits left behind as water rushes through, constantly wear down certain areas and build up other areas.

There are three major waterfalls in Havasu Canyon– Navajo, Havasu and Mooney falls. About a mile and a half downstream from Supai is Navajo Falls, named after a famous Havasupai chief who died in 1898. The appearance of Navajo Falls has changed several times in the recent past due to the forces of erosion. Currently, it is divided roughly into two equal areas. One is a steep cascade while the other is a single stream that leaps free of the canyon wall and falls freely for about 75 feet.

Two miles below the village is Havasu Falls, which leaps through a notch in the travertine rim of the canyon and spills into a turquoise pool not quite 100 feet below. This waterfall has also been called "Bridal Veil Falls." Havasu Falls is known around the world for its beauty and the travertine dams formed below the fall. At one time, Havasu Falls was surveyed to be one 125 feet high. This was undoubtedly conducted before the current break in the wall.

The highest waterfall in Havasu Canyon is Mooney Falls, located three miles below Supai. Named for prospector James Mooney who fell to his death here in 1880, the pool below Mooney Falls is the largest pool in the canyon. Walls of the surrounding canyon are higher here than those at Havasu or Navajo Falls. Havasu Creek plunges 196 feet from the top of Mooney Falls into the pool below.

Vegetation surrounding Mooney Falls is more lush and the natural amphitheater's walls have more color and texture than any others found in the canyon. Although it is difficult to reach Mooney Falls, the effort is well spent.

Left: Venus maidenhair vern and delicate moss spring to life in precarious positions along the banks of Havasu Creek.
PHOTO BY CHARLES CHANLEY

Right: Navajo Falls, named for Havasupai chief Navajo who died in 1898, has changed appearance several times in the recent past as floods coursed through the canyon.
PHOTO BY CHARLES CHANLEY

Following pages: Havasu Falls is known world-wide for its beauty and the natural travertine dams that form below the falls.
PHOTO BY CHARLES CHANLEY

THE INNER CANYON

The Inner Canyon provides the environment for a varied riparian, or streamside, community. Here, a lack of water is not the overwhelming obstacle for plant and animal life it becomes in other regions of the Grand Canyon.

For more adventurous visitors, the Inner Canyon offers a uniquely rewarding experience. Lying some 3000 feet below the Canyon's rims, the Tonto Platform is the basis for the broad Benchlands extending from Marble Canyon through the central Grand Canyon. In the western regions of the Canyon the Tonto Platform is less developed and joins with the Esplanade to form two wide terraces that are the Benchlands major landforms.

The Tonto Platform was created as weaker layers of the Bright Angel Shale were eroded, leaving the more resistant Tapeats Sandstone to form a base for the resulting benchlands. In some places these broad terraces are as much as three miles wide. The resulting area, with elevations generally between 3000 and 4000 feet, has a semi-arid climate and supports a Desert Scrub Community.

The Esplanade is the major terrace in the western Canyon, occurring at elevations approximately 1000 feet higher than the Tonto Platform. The Esplanade was created as layers of Hermit Shale were stripped away leaving more erosion resistant Supai Sandstone. With elevations between 4000 and 5000 feet, the Esplanade has a semi-arid climate and has vegetation representative of both Desert Scrub and Piñon-Juniper Woodland communities.

The Inner Canyon is home to the Colorado River and its tributaries. Here, an entirely different world awaits. As the Colorado flows through the 277.7 miles of the Grand Canyon from Lee's Ferry to Lake Mead, it drops more than 1900 feet in elevation, an average of more than seven feet per mile, with much steeper gradients in rapids. The Inner Canyon has 161 recognized rapids, a number that fluctuates depending on the flow of waters released upstream. Construction of Glen Canyon Dam in 1963 has been instrumental in controlling the flow of water through the Grand Canyon. Although not popular with all interests from an environmental standpoint, Glen Canyon Dam has been a key factor in controlling the sometimes erratic Colorado.

The width of the Colorado averages between 200 and 300 feet as it flows through the Grand Canyon and reaches its narrowest point, in Granite Narrows, at 60 feet. The depth of the river varies throughout the Canyon, depending in large measure on the water flow released from Glen Canyon Dam. On average, its depth is approximately 50 feet, with the deepest point at 110 feet. Average flow of the water through the Canyon is 4.2 miles per hour, with the rapids flowing as fast as 10 miles per hour.

The Canyon floor provides the environment water is not the overwhelming obstacle for plant and animal life it is in other regions of the Canyon. Along the banks of the Colorado life flourishes as the river cuts its way into rock foundations of the Precambrian era. The continuing story of the Canyon, and the river, continues to unfold as the years pass.

Left: The springs at Vasey's Paradise, named by the John Wesley Powell expedition of 1869 for botanist George W. Vasey, pour from the Redwall Limestone cliffs of Marble Gorge.
PHOTO BY TOM TILL

Right: A present day explorer approaches Crystal Rapid in Granite Gorge. Between Powell's 1869 river run and 1949 only 100 people, including Powell's crews, had boated through the Canyon. By the mid-1970s, more than 100 times that amount ran the river annually.
PHOTO BY LARRY ULRICH

Right: Sunlight filters into the interior of Deer Creek Gorge near its junction with the Colorado River in the Inner Canyon.
PHOTO BY TOM TILL

Left: Char Butte towers above the turquoise waters of the Little Colorado River. The Little Colorado River flows into the Colorado River at the south end of Marble Canyon.
PHOTO BY LARRY ULRICH

Right: Maidenhair fern, scarlet monkeyflower and delicate moss form hanging gardens in Elves Chasm on Royal Arch Creek.
PHOTO BY LARRY ULRICH

Following pages: A golden sunset illuminates the Benchlands of the Esplanade near Havasu Canyon. The Esplanade averages between 4000 and 5000 feet in elevation and is as much as five miles wide in places.
PHOTO BY GARY LADD

Outside back cover: Snow blankets Mather Point after a winter snowstorm.
PHOTO BY JERRY SIEVE